60 DAY DEVOTIONAL

VOLUME 1

Minister Leon Johnson ● Diamond Johnson

Daily Reflections for Faith, Growth, and Purpose

Copyright © 2026 LifeTime Inspirations Ministries
All rights reserved.
No part of this publication may be reproduced, stored in a retrieval system, transmitted, or distributed in any form or by any means—electronic, mechanical, photocopying, recording, scanning, or otherwise—except as permitted under Sections 107 or 108 of the United States Copyright Act, without the prior written permission of the Publisher.
Scripture quotations are taken from the Holy Bible, including the
New King James Version (NKJV),
© 1982 by Thomas Nelson, Inc.;
the New International Version (NIV),
© 1978, 1984, 2011 by Biblica, Inc.;
and the Amplified® Bible (AMP),
© 2015 by The Lockman Foundation.
Used by permission. All rights reserved.
This publication is designed for spiritual formation, discipleship, and ministry-based activation. The content is provided for inspirational and educational purposes and is not intended to replace pastoral counsel, professional advice, or individualized spiritual guidance.

Published by:
LifeTime Inspirations Ministries
Printed in the United States of America.

ISBN: 979-8-9946446-0-7

Purchase of this publication does not grant permission to reproduce, distribute, facilitate, or license the material for group, church-wide, or commercial use without prior written authorization from the Publisher.

BEFORE DIVING IN...

Unlock the Volume 1 Companion Resource Hub

This companion hub was created to support the devotional you're holding—offering clarity, encouragement, and optional guidance along the way. Inside, you'll find simple direction for using the devotional, insight on journaling, and ways individuals or groups can engage without pressure or expectations.

Scan the QR Code, type the URL into your browser, or click the link (in the eBook) to enter the Companion Resource Hub: https://subscribepage.io/volume1resourcehub

FOREWORD

Our deepest fear is not that we are inadequate; our deepest fear is that we are POWERFUL beyond measure... - Marianne Williamson

Leon Johnson, widowed after 32 years of Marriage to his amazing wife Donna Ritchie Johnson, she was truly the apple of his eye. To hear him ever speak of her and their relationship brings to mind and heart that feeling you have as a little girl, when you think of "and they lived happily ever after" It's the resounding love, respect and adoration, one only dreams of, personified for countless to witness in the marriage of Leon and Donna.

I share this account because LifeTime Inspirations is the continuation of the work Donna began. Leon was summoned by God in August, 2017 to continue the daily inspirations. As he recounts" I believe in all of my heart, this is one of those destiny moments, doing what you were called to do"

FOREWORD

Leon, embracing His destiny has led him, unbeknownst to him, to help many others embrace their destiny, living in their God given purpose on purpose. Thank Mr. Johnson for allowing God to use you to remind me that Nothing in all Creation can separate me from God's Love. With God Leading my efforts, Nothing can stop me...

"Nothing Can Separate You from the Love of Christ... NOTHING"

"Nothing Can Stop Me... I'm All the Way Up" – Artist Infared

It was once told to me in the sweetest simplicity, "Ky you are afraid of your own Greatness." Every time you see God elevating you to a space, a place that is out of your comfort zone, you shrink back... As I reflected on my life over the past 30+ years, I could only concur.

FOREWORD

Choosing Excellence in your own life first, and then in the lives of others you align yourself with, promotes greater scrutiny, responsibility, and accountability. My fear did not come from the inevitable critique of others, but more so of the unrelenting analysis I continually imposed upon and within myself.

Enveloped by self-doubt, and internally anguished by the haunting echoes of what I would never be, by those I loved, immobilized me at varying stages throughout my life. BUT GOD... My Lord and Savior rescued me, reminded me, inspired me, propelled me, in a word LOVED me.

God used the Daily LifeTime Inspirations of My Dear Friend and Brother in Christ Leon Johnson to breathe Life into me, to pull me up and through. Strengthening me to WALK in my Purpose.

FOREWORD

Romans 8:28-31, 35, 37-39 New International Version (NIV)

28 And we know that in all things God works for the good of those who love him, who have been called according to his purpose. **29** For those God foreknew he also predestined to be conformed to the image of his Son, that he might be the firstborn among many brothers and sisters. **30** And those he predestined, he also called; those he called, he also justified; those he justified, he also glorified.
31 What, then, shall we say in response to these things? If God is for us, who can be against us?...
35 Who shall separate us from the love of Christ? Shall trouble or hardship or persecution or famine or nakedness or danger or sword? ...
... **37** No, in all these things we are more than conquerors through him who loved us. **38** For I am convinced that neither death nor life, neither angels nor demons, neither the present nor the future, nor any powers,

FOREWORD

39 neither height nor depth, nor anything else in all creation, will be able to separate us from the love of God that is in Christ Jesus our Lord.

I am tremendously grateful to LifeTime Inspirations, for aiding in my healing and growth spiritually. I am convinced that I would not have experienced spiritual evolution personally or professionally without the daily infusion of these inspirations.

In His Love,
    Kyri Isaac, PhD, MEd, CHC

TO ASSIST YOU IN YOUR 60-DAY JOURNEY:

Unlock the Guided Reflections for Individuals

This gentle companion offers quiet moments of stillness, prayer, and Scripture-centered reflection as you move through the 60-Day Devotional. Designed to support—not replace—your devotional reading or journal, this guide helps you slow down, listen deeply, and align your heart to both the Word and the devotional messages.

Scan the QR Code, type the URL into your browser, or click the link (in the eBook) to download the Guided Reflections PDF.

https://subscribepage.io/volume1guidedreflections

DAY 1

What Season Are You In? God Has an Appointed Time for You

"There is a season (a time appointed) for everything and a time for every delight and event or purpose under heaven —" (Ecclesiastes 3:1)

What season are you in right now? A fruit tree knows that in its right season, it is time to bear fruit. The same happens for you. There is a time for planting, watering, and waiting.

When it is your season, you will bear much fruit. You have to be faithful in the waiting period. So, keep doing the right thing. Trust God in His timing with the right attitude.

"But his delight is in the law of the LORD. And on His law [His precepts and teachings] he [habitually] meditates day and night. And he will be like a tree firmly planted [and fed] by streams of water, which yields its fruit in its season; whose leaf does not wither; and in whatever he does, he prospers [and comes to maturity]." (Psalms 1:2-3)

I declare you are about to enter into your season of more blessings, in Jesus' Name!

DAY 2

We Are Better Together

God has ordained people to be in your life who will strengthen you, encourage you, and push you toward your purpose.

Hebrews 10:25 says, *"Forsake not the assembling of yourselves together."*

Together we are better, stronger, smarter, and more powerful! Don't waste another year doing life solo. The scripture says, *"When we come together in unity, there is a commanded blessing." (Psalms 133:1-3)*

DAY 3

God's Got This

We all have things that come against us and experience things we don't understand. It's easy to live uptight wondering how everything is going to work out.

If we're not careful, we'll get discouraged, live worried, and not believe things are going to change.

But there's a simple phrase you have to get down in your spirit - "God's got this."

Keep your peace, because you have God's favor. Let go and let God work it out for you.

Be still and know that He is God, because: God's got this!

DAY 4

Don't Give Up On The Promises Of God

We all have opportunities to give up on what God promised us. This attitude causes us to walk away from uncomfortable situations.

But God wants to show you why it's important to not give up on the promises He put in your heart; or on the hearts of people He's placed in your life. Learn the importance of loyalty and faithfulness and how they tie into your destiny.

Elisha received a double portion of Elijah's anointing when he stayed committed until the end of Elijah's life. In the same way, if you want to walk in the fullness of God's blessing and receive everything God has for you, you have to stay committed to the dreams God has placed in your heart.

Stay committed to the people He put in your life that will help you on your way to success!

I believe in you; and God does also!

DAY 5

Trust God to Fight For You

Whatever is trying to stop you - a mountain of debt, sickness, depression or addiction - may look insurmountable. But, it's no match for our God.

God told the Israelites in Isaiah 45:2, *"I will go before you and level the mountains."* The Most High God is going before you today and fighting your battles.

Are you living worried, stressed out, and trying to figure out how your situation is going to work out? The good news is that you're not on your own. God is saying, "Trust Me. I have you covered. I know where you are and where you are going."

One touch of His favor will turn that mountain into level ground.

DAY 6

Trust God In Everything

God will never give you a purpose that He has not already prepared you for.

Anything that has come against you has a designed purpose for your growth. In Joshua 1:6-9 God tells Joshua to *"be strong and very courageous"* several times and to meditate on His word day and night.

God is telling us that He will go before us to fight our battles.

If we do what His word says, we will prosper and have good success. God's formula is simple: all we have to do is trust in Him and He will make the crooked places straight.

We serve an amazing God!

DAY 7

God Is Your Lawyer

Has someone judged you, spread rumors about you, or hurt you?

Our human nature naturally wants to set the record straight and prove that those who've wronged us are wrong. But, all it does is take up valuable energy and can keep us from being everything God has created us to be.

Instead, God wants to be your defender. In Jeremiah 51:36, God says to us, *"I will defend you. I will be your lawyer. I will plead your case."*

You don't have to defend yourself. You have a Defender. The Most High God said He will settle your cases. Live with more freedom, joy and peace as you let God fight your battles. Trust Him to protect your reputation against every unfair word.

No weapon formed against you will prosper!

My God is bad to the bone! What a Mighty God we serve!

DAY 8

Get in Agreement with God's Word

Are you ready to give up on what you're believing for because all you've heard is "NO"? Well, it's time to get ready because "YES" is coming!

No matter who has said "no" or how many times a door has closed, God has already set a date to bring His promises to pass in your life. But there is one thing God needs from you: your "YES".

2 Corinthians 1 says, *"God's yes and our yes together make a sure thing."* Your faith will grow as you hear amazing stories from the Bible of men and women who dared to believe God for a yes and saw amazing breakthroughs. You, too, will receive your own breakthrough as you say Yes with God!

"If one can chase a thousand, two can put ten thousand to flight..." (Deuteronomy 32:30)

Now there are three: me, you, and God!

DAY 9

Do You Know Who You Are in Christ?

In Genesis 1, the first thing that God says about you and me is that He created us in His image.

Having His image and likeness inside of us was meant to be our source of strength and confidence.

The question is, have you allowed the enemy and things that have happened to you to distort the image of God in your life?

You need to get your true image back!

1. You are a child of God
2. You were born to succeed
3. You are joint heirs with Christ
4. You are victorious
5. You are highly favored
6. You are blessed
7. You are successful
8. You are prosperous
9. You walk in divine healing
10. You are a friend of God

God really loves you; and so do I.

DAY 10

Finish Strong! God is Not Through with You Yet

God has already finished the work in you. Now it is time for you to come into agreement with Him and stop letting distractions hold you back in fulfilling your destiny.

Instead of accepting an addiction as a part of your life and allowing it to stay, you need to announce to that addiction, "It is finished! You don't control me, and you can't keep me from my destiny. The price has been paid. I am free. I am whole. I am clean."

When you rise up, tell the past, tell the poverty, tell the guilt, "It is finished!"

"This is not who I am. I am blessed. I am prosperous. I am victorious!"

Strongholds are broken in the unseen realm, chains are loosed, and favor is released!

You and God are a majority. There is nothing that is standing in your way, except you. God will always direct you, but you have to let Him do it.

Let go and let God!

DAY 11

Stay Faithful

Are you faithful in the small things and things that seem to be routine?

One test we all have to pass is being faithful in the ordinary days. Like clay spinning on the wheel, sometimes our lives can feel like we are spinning and not getting anywhere. It's like we're just doing the same thing every day.

It's easy to feel like giving up and losing momentum when nothing is happening. Like that clay on a potter's wheel, when it feels like you're going in circles, something is happening that you can't see. You're growing. Behind the scenes, God is making and molding you, preparing you for where He wants to take you. But, you have to stay on His Potter's Wheel and stay faithful!

Even the great Bible heroes faced ordinary days and routine. When you are faithful on average days, then you will see exceptional days. You will learn to enjoy where God has you right now so you'll never miss out on the new things God has in store!

Stay faithful in the small things and God will bless you in the big things.

DAY 12

PSALM 23
The Lord Is My Shepherd

Let's take a look at how beautiful the message is in Psalm 23. For our Reflection!

The Lord is My Shepherd
* This is relationship!! *

I will not want anything
* This is supply!! *

In places of green pastures it makes me rest
* This is rest!!

Resting waters beside me
* This is Caution!! *

He restores my soul
* This is Health!! *

He guides me on paths of justice
* This is Address!! *

DAY 12

PSALM 23
The Lord Is My Shepherd (part 2)

For the sake of his name.
* This is Purpose!! *

Even though I pass through the valley of the shadow of death
* This is Test!! *

I will fear no evil
* This is Faith!! *

Because you are with me
* This is Fidelity!! *

Your rod and your staff give me breath.
* This is Hope !! *

You prepare a table in front of me.
* This is Provision!! *

In the presence of my enemies;
* This is Protection!! *

DAY 12

PSALM 23
The Lord Is My Shepherd (part 3, final)

You have anointed my head with oil;
* This is Consecration!! *

My cup is overflowing.
* This is Abundance!! *

Surely goodness and mercy shall follow me all the days of my life.
* This is Blessing!! *

And in the house of the Lord I will dwell
* This is Promise!! *

For long days.
* This is Eternity!! *

Pass this Blessing!!

God blesses you so that you can pass this blessing to everyone you know.

DAY 13

Blessings In Dark Seasons

We all go through times that we don't understand. But Matthew 5:45 tells us, *"Rain falls on the just and the unjust."* This means we are all going to go through dark seasons and face difficult times. God wants to show you how to face these dark seasons with hope and the right attitude.

Our dark seasons always lead us to the amazing things God has in store for our future. The Psalmist said in Psalm 112:4, *"When darkness overtakes the righteous, light will come bursting in."* You can have hope during your darkest hours.

Don't let the dark seasons convince you that you've seen your best days.

You wouldn't be alive if God didn't have something amazing in front of you. Without the dark seasons, we wouldn't become everything we were created to be.

Gomer Pyle had it right. He always said "Look on the bright side!"

DAY 14

Where Is Your Confidence?

Sometimes in life you may feel down and have lost all confidence in the God-given capabilities that He Blessed you with.

No one can take your confidence - except you give it away. God wanted me to tell you to take your confidence back!

Listen to what the word of God said in Hebrews 13:6: *"So that we may boldly say, The Lord is my helper, and I will not fear what shall man do unto me?"*

Don't let people nor the devil steal your confidence. Know who you are in Christ!

You will accomplish all that God has called you to do and more, in Jesus' Name!

DAY 15

God Is Not Ashamed of You

God is not ashamed of you. He knows everything about you. He's reaching out to you with love.

Like the lady at the well, Jesus knew all about this lady and all of her issues. But, Jesus never condemned or judged her. Neither is He judging you. His love for us is so amazing, even when we make mistakes.

So, hold your head up, put your shoulders back, and walk upright with confidence. With God by your side, you can accomplish your dreams in Jesus' name.

Like the apostle Paul said, *"I am not ashamed of the Gospel of Jesus Christ."* (Romans 1:16)

And guess what?

He is not ashamed of you either!

DAY 16

God Goes Before Us

Are you facing a mountain today? Whatever is aiming to stop you and block you cannot outmatch God! God told the Israelites in Isaiah 45:2 *"I will go before you and level the mountains."* The Most High God is going before you today and fighting your battles. He's making the crooked places straight.

If you're constantly living in fear or anxiety, take heart today! God is saying, "Trust Me. I have you covered. I know where you are and where you're going." One touch of His favor will turn that mountain into level ground.

God wants to make you an example of His blessings for all to see. And when they do, they will know it was the hand of God. Just like when He raised Lazarus from the dead, everyone knew it was the Hand and Favor of God.

You are coming into your land of increase and promotion; great favor and prosperity; and great health and wealth, in Jesus' Name!

And it's all thanks to God, Who goes before you and causes you to rise and prosper in everything you do.

DAY 17

Run Your Own Race and Stay in Peace

Are you living a life of peace? To live in peace is to live a life of rest. Hebrews 4:11 tells us to *"make every effort to enter into the rest of God"*. What this means is that we have to actively guard our peace.

You see, life is full of Peace Stealers.

Every day, people and circumstances will try to pull you out of your place of rest. You need to put up boundaries and not allow everything in. You need to identify the Peace Stealers in your life and learn how to take care of your emotional energy.

Even in the midst of difficulties and trials, learn how God wants to fight your battles for you! All you need to do is rest in Him!

Don't let people control you. You can miss your destiny trying to keep them happy. God wants you to totally trust in Him, so He can lead and guide you. Therefore, all you need to do is rest and let God fight your battles. He wants the best for you because you are His child!

Have a super blessed Day, in Jesus' Name!

DAY 18

My Soul Is Anchored In The Lord

There will always be something trying to get us to pull up our anchor of hope—bad breaks, delays, disappointments, etc. In these tough times, when life doesn't make sense, when your prayers haven't been answered as quickly as you'd like - it's easy to throw in the towel and give up. But, you have to make sure to keep your anchor down and hope in the Lord.

When you're anchored to hope, God will make things happen that you could never make happen on your own. When you have your hope in Him, the scripture says you'll never be disappointed. You may have some temporary setbacks. But when it's all said and done, you'll come out better than you were before if you don't give up your hope!

One of greatest psalmists of our time, Douglas Miller, wrote a great song: *"My Soul is anchored in the Lord"*. When you feel down, pull up that song and let it minister to your soul. All through the scriptures, men and women of faith were tested. But, they put their anchors down and trusted in God.

Keep the faith! What God started in your life, He will fulfill and bring to pass. The plans He has for your life and the dreams He gave you will be accomplished, in Jesus' Name!

DAY 19

Keep The Joy in Your Life

Have you allowed the pressures of life to weigh you down to where you're not laughing as much as you used to? Have you stopped enjoying life?

While every person deals with stress and challenges, if we're not careful, it's very easy to - one day - look up and find that we don't smile as much, we're not as friendly, and the joy of life has disappeared.

God wants to show you how you can live without heaviness no matter the circumstances. Jesus said in John 16:33, *"In life you will have difficulties, but be of good cheer."* Let this message show you how to get your joy back. As you make this important shift, you'll feel stronger, younger and fresher.

You'll have the strength to finish your course with joy!
If you don't have fun or you're not smiling, you need to notify your face because most people's expressions seem sad all the time. Put laughter back inside of you and smile more.

This promotes healing and good health. Hang around people that bring joy in your life. Laughter is spiritual warfare, laughter tears down walls. Laughter brings joy for you, your family, and all those that are around you.

Have a fun-filled day, in Jesus' Name!

DAY 20

Wait on the Lord so You Can Soar with Eagles

There are times in life that we all get tired: tired of trying to make a business grow, tired of dealing with a sickness, tired of raising a difficult child, tired of living lonely, and tired of waiting to meet the right person.

But Isaiah 40:31 says, *"But those who hope in the Lord will renew their strength. They will soar on wings like eagles; they will run and not grow weary, they will walk and not be faint."* Wait upon the Lord and hope in Him. Don't give up when victory is right around the corner.

God promises He will renew your strength.

As you continue to walk with God, He will lead you into your destiny and fulfill every desire and need. Hang around Eagles so you can soar like an eagle. Eagles dwell in very high places. They know who they are. You should know who you are also. You are a child of the Most High God who sits in heavenly places; who will guide you into your destiny to stand before kings and walk upright and proud. You are the child of the King of Kings!

Have a blessed day; and I will see you at the top!

DAY 21

Are You Looking Back in the Past or Looking Forward Towards the Future?

You can count on this – the past ended one second ago.

From this point onward, you can be clean, filled with His Spirit, and used in many different ways for His honor. *"If they listen and obey God, they will be blessed with prosperity throughout their lives. All their years will be pleasant." Job 36:11*

After all that Job went through, he had a decision to make. Was he going to look at the past and all that he was going through? Or was he going to look forward? He decided to look forward and have a victor mentality. God rewarded him more than double from what he used to have.

It is always amazing to me that everyone has the same opportunities to fulfill their God given dreams. Some go half way and stop. But, winners keep moving forward. I believe you are a winner and nothing is impossible for you because if God is for you, no one can stop your destiny from being fulfilled, in Jesus' Name!

DAY 22

Don't Look to People. Look to God!

Everyone can trust God with every outcome. We don't have to manipulate situations. We don't have to be defiant or try to figure out how to always win. Our responsibility is to trust God and leave all the consequences to Him.

"In this act we see what real love is: it is not our love for God, but His love for us, when He sent His Son to satisfy God's anger against our sins."
1 John 4:10
(The Living Bible)

God loves us more than we love ourselves. Stay faithful in the word of God. In Joshua 1:8, God said for us to meditate on His word day and night, for *"then thou shall make thy way prosperous and thou shall have good success".* God sends blessings our way. It is up to us to receive them.

God is turning things around for you right now, in Jesus' Name!

DAY 23

Is Your Love for God Growing on Purpose in Your Life?

Just as people grow and their lives change, we have to adapt our love to those changes. Our love has to mature and grow.

This is so important that the Apostle Paul prayed for the Church in Philippi: *"And this is my prayer: that your love may abound more and more in knowledge and depth of insight"* (Philippians 1:9 NIV).

It wasn't that the church was deficient in love, but Paul was saying, "Your love has so much potential to go so much further and build a greater foundation in your lives. Agree with me every day as I pray for you that your love will reach its fullest."

The greatest commandment is for us to love one another.

Have a super blessed day, in Jesus' Name!

DAY 24

Who, or What, Are You Depending On?

When we depend on organizations, we get what organizations can do. When we depend on education, we get what education can do. When we depend on man, we get what man can do. But when we depend on prayer, we get what God can do.

"Everyone who believes that Jesus is the Christ has been born of God, and everyone who loves the Father loves whoever has been born of him."
1 John 5:1 (The English Standard Version)

You are on your way to unexpected blessings because your trust is in God.

Have a beautifully blessed day, in Jesus' Name!

DAY 25

You Can Overcome Weariness

As we go through life's many seasons, it's easy to grow tired and weary. But when we are weary, we don't enjoy the greatest blessings in our lives like we should.

Galatians 6:9 encourages us, *"Let us not become weary in doing good, for at the proper time we will reap a harvest if we do not give up."*

Find refreshment and motivation to keep on going. Stay renewed and inspired no matter what you may be facing today. Discover how to have balance physically, spiritually and emotionally so you'll have the strength to be a blessing to others and accomplish your life purpose full of peace and joy.

Don't let people steal your joy. Get around positive people that will encourage you to move forward. And if you don't have anyone to stand with you, encourage yourself.

You are the righteousness of God Almighty! He will guide your every step, in Jesus' Name!

DAY 26

The Power of Agreement

The Bible says when believers dwell together in unity, *"there the LORD commanded the blessing—life forevermore."* (Psalm 133:3).

It is only the love of God that brings people to the arms and saving power of Jesus Christ. God is saying that it's up to us to keep in unity and in the bond of peace.

The Bible also says, *"if one should chase a thousand, two can put ten thousand to flight."* (Deuteronomy 32:30)

There is so much power in agreement that is available to us if we simply touch and agree. So, let us stand together in unity so God can do amazing things in our lives.

I pray many blessings for you, your family, and all of your brothers and sisters in Christ.

DAY 27

Do You Have a Giving Heart?

Once in an age, God sends to some of us a friend who truly loves us. Not the man or woman that we are, but the angel we may be.
Our lives will always be full if our hearts are always giving.

"For if we are faithful to the end, trusting God just as we did when we first became Christians, we will share in all that belongs to Christ."
(Hebrews 3:14)
The Living Bible

Continue to be a blessing to all who you meet and love. As you continue to give, God will open up the windows of heaven that no man can shut. Find someone who you can bless today and watch God move on your behalf.

Your needs will be taken care of by God, because you blessed someone less fortunate than yourself.

I pray many blessings upon you, in Jesus' Name!

DAY 28

Be A Giver and Learn How to Be Blessed

"Let us hold fast the confession of our hope without wavering, for He who promised is faithful."
Hebrews 10:23

Giving is not an economic decision – it's a spiritual one! The need to give is out of our substance rather than our surplus; from our hearts and not our heads.

God sees your heart. Once you understand the power of giving, you will understand the blessing in receiving. Years ago, my mother-in-law taught me a very important principle on receiving. She told me, "When you don't accept blessings others are trying to give to you, you cut off their blessings."

Ever since then, I learned to receive all that God has for me.

You are blessed to be a blessing! Now, start receiving the commanded blessings in your life, in Jesus' Name!

DAY 29

You Have Victory In Christ

He who loses control of his thoughts will lose control of his actions.

God will take you through the fire, through the storm, and through the lion's den. But as long as you put your trust in God, you can rest assured that you will be victorious.

In Psalm 27, listen to what David said (and you need to say this also):
"The Lord is my light and my salvation; whom shall I fear? The Lord is the strength of my life; of whom shall I be afraid? When the wicked, even mine enemies and my foes, came upon me to eat up my flesh, they stumbled and fell. Though a host should encamp against me, my heart shall not fear: though war should rise against me, in this will I be confident. One thing have I desired of the Lord, that will I seek after; that I may dwell in the house of the Lord all the days of my life, to behold the beauty of the Lord, and to enquire in his temple. For in the time of trouble he shall hide me in his pavilion: in the secret of his tabernacle shall he hide me; he shall set me up upon a rock. And now shall mine head be lifted up above mine enemies round about me: therefore will I offer in his tabernacle sacrifices of joy; I will sing, yea, I will sing praises unto the Lord."

The victory is yours, in Jesus' Name!

DAY 30

Look Beyond the Bad and Remember God's Promises

"Knowing this, that the trying of your faith worketh patience." (James 1:2-4)

Reach boldly for the miracle! God knows your gifts, your hindrances, and the condition you are in at every moment.

Are you judging the rest of your life by the season you're in now? Every person has unfair seasons, slow seasons, and discouraging seasons. But, you have to remind yourself during these times, "it is just a season." It's not the rest of your life. This too shall pass.
Learn to stay in faith and keep the right perspective in adversity. Whenever you feel stretched, know you're in position to be propelled. God uses the difficulty to push you into new levels. The more you get pulled back, the more you're going to shoot forward.

Faith and obedience are inescapably related. There is no saving faith in God apart from obedience to God. As such, there can be no godly obedience without godly faith.

Keep the faith, because God is about to surge you forward, in Jesus' Name!

PAUSE HERE FOR A MOMENT

Unlock The 60-Day Devotional Activation: Audio Reflections

These 7 short audio reflections are designed to help you slow down, settle your heart, and stay aligned as you move through the 60-day devotional. Each track reinforces simple rhythms—Scripture, prayer, reflection, obedience, and consistency—without pressure or performance.

Scan the QR Code, type the URL into your browser, or click the link (in the eBook) to listen and continue your devotional journey with gentle guidance.

https://subscribepage.io/audioreflections

DAY 31

Your Rewards Are In God

It's easy to go through life trying to impress people, to show them that we are strong, that we have it all together. But if you'll humble yourself, empty out your pride, your fear, and your doubts and get real, God will help you to grow. You'll come up higher.

In this crazy world, there's an enormous distinction between good times and bad, between sorrow and joy. But in the eyes of God, they're never separated. Where there is pain, there is healing. Where there is mourning, there is dancing. Where there is poverty, there is the kingdom.

"And whatsoever ye do in word or deed, do all in the name of the Lord Jesus, giving thanks to God and the Father by him..." (Colossians 3:17)

"And whatsoever ye do, do it heartily, as to the Lord, and not unto men; Knowing that of the Lord ye shall receive the reward of the inheritance: for ye serve the Lord Christ." (Colossians 3:23-24)

You and God are a majority.

DAY 32

When You Pray, Just Believe

The Psalmist said in Psalm 56:9, *"The moment you pray, the tide of the battle turns."* In the unseen realm, God begins to change things in your favor the moment you pray. But many times, when we've been praying for a long time for something, and don't see anything happening in the natural, it can seem like God went on vacation and our prayers aren't doing any good.

But even when you can't see behind the scenes, God is at work. He not only heard you when you prayed, but He took it one step further; He put the miracle in motion. Just because you don't see anything happening doesn't mean the answer is not on the way. The people that see breakthroughs and promises fulfilled are the people that keep praying, keep believing and keep standing in faith. The word of God will inspire and equip you to be one of those people!

Here is what God tells us to do:
"For verily I say unto you, That whosoever shall say unto this mountain, Be thou removed, and be thou cast into the sea; and shall not doubt in his heart, but shall believe that those things which he saith shall come to pass; he shall have whatsoever he saith. Therefore I say unto you, what things soever ye desire, when ye pray, believe that ye receive them, and ye shall have them."
(Mark 11:23-24)

Keep saying what God said about you.

Prayer + Believing = Success and a Prosperous fulfilled Destiny.

DAY 33

Get Wisdom

"For the Lord giveth wisdom: out of his mouth cometh knowledge and understanding." (Proverbs 2:6)

"If any of you lack wisdom, let him ask of God, that giveth to all men liberally, and upbraideth not; and it shall be given him." (James 1:5)

I heard about a man that went to a machine shop to fix a piece of equipment at a plant. He took out his hammer and tapped the equipment and it started working. He sent them a bill for $1000 and the plant manager said, I saw what you did to fix it and why is the bill so high? The plant manager demanded an itemized bill. So the guy broke the bill down. It was $1 for me to take my hammer out of my bag, and it cost $999 to know exactly where to tap.

So my question to you is, are you tapping into people that cannot lead you to your destiny or are you tapping into people that are already where you need to be. In other words, if you are broke, and your desire is to be wealthy or have enough to help someone else, then why do you hang around broke people? The Bible says. How can the blind lead the blind, except they fall into the ditch? It should be a goal for all to be what God called us to be so we can help those that are less fortunate and bring them to a higher level.

Be blessed so you can bless others, in Jesus' Name!

DAY 34

Sometimes you have to Encourage Yourself

"And David was greatly distressed; for the people spoke of stoning him, because the souls of all the people were grieved, every man for his sons and for his daughters: but David encouraged himself in the Lord his God." (1 Samuel 30:6)

How do you know when people need encouragement?

If they have life in their body, everyone needs encouragement, but sometimes you have to encourage yourself like David.

One thing for you to consider every day, "If you value people and show that you believe in them, they will unconditionally be drawn to you".

Love never fails!

Lift up your brother and sister in Christ, in Jesus' Name, everyday!

DAY 35

Your thinking needs to line up with the Word of God

In Proverbs 23-7, the Bible says: *"For as he thinketh in his heart, so is he: Eat and drink, saith he to thee; but his heart is not with thee."*

When you are in emotional pain, it's easy to shrink back in fear and allow an emotional limp to become a stronghold in your mind—a wrong way of thinking. The last thing you want to do is to step out in boldness or put yourself in a position where you can get hurt again.

But you can't allow a painful experience to trick you into thinking you're going to have a painful life. If you find yourself shrinking back because you are afraid you will be hurt again, you have to understand that God can heal what hurts! He is the mender of broken hearts. We serve a mighty God.

If you think about lack, you will have lack. If you think about success, you will be successful. So, it is important that you think and say the right things all the time.

Start speaking what God says about you, because you are a child of the King!

DAY 36

Be Still and Know

God doesn't remove every frustration in our lives. In fact, many of the things that frustrate us, God uses to grow us and take us to the next level.

You need to live in peace no matter your circumstance. Learn how to deal with difficult people, let go of the approval of others, and run your race strong, focused, and unshakeable!

The Scripture says in Psalm 46:10, *"Be still and know that I am God."*

As you learn to let go and let God, you will enjoy your life more and become everything He has created you to be, in Jesus' name!

DAY 37

God Sends Opportunities Your Way

"We wait in hope for the LORD; he is our help and our shield."
(Psalm 33:20)

There is only one you. God wanted you to be you. Don't you dare change just because you're outnumbered! You have to trust that God will put the right people in your life at the right time and for the right reasons.

Opportunities will come your way, so you need to make the most of the opportunities right in front of you, and even better opportunities will begin to chase you down.

"Success occurs when opportunity meets preparation."

You are a winner, in Jesus' Name!

DAY 38

Building Trust In Our Relationship with Others

The Bible says this in Jeremiah 17:7 about trust: *"Blessed is the man that trusteth in the Lord, and whose hope the Lord is."*

If you want to have a great life, enough people must say that they need you in their lives.

Be Authentic...be someone other people trust...and use the opportunity to interpret your own value.

You must see yourself as God sees you. As you put your trust completely in Christ, others will follow because they see the blessings in your life.

"And we know that all things work together for good to them that love God, to them who are called according to his purpose." (Romans 8:28)

Have a super blessed day, in Jesus' Name!

DAY 39

Your Blessings are Closer Than you Think

"Don't be afraid, for I am with you. Don't be discouraged, for I am your God. I will strengthen you and help you. I will hold you up with my victorious right hand."
(Isaiah 41:10)

O Holy Spirit of God, abide with us; inspire all our thoughts; pervade our imaginations; suggest all our decisions; order all our doings.

This is a great prayer!

Trust God to direct every step and to speak through us that every word has power and wisdom and clear direction.

A spiritual secret is to learn contentment with the things God doesn't explain to us.

It is for our own good that some things we are praying for don't come to pass, because our thinking may be too small and God has something bigger and greater in mind that will launch you into your destiny. He wants to bless you with the Ephesians 3:20 blessing - more than you can ask or imagine.

So get ready for your blessings, because it is closer than you think!

DAY 40

Give Yourself

"Give, and it shall be given unto you; good measure, pressed down, and shaken together, and running over, shall men give into your bosom. For with the same measure that ye mete withal it shall be measured to you again." (Luke 6:38)

Most people only look at this scripture when it deals with money. But what if you don't have money, then you should give yourself. I am reminded that while the church offering was taken, everyone gave their finances, but one person had nothing, so he put himself in the offering basket.

So who do you think gave the most? The one that had nothing, gave his all.

God wants all of you. The giving of your finances is an act of obedience and releases the promises He made to us, but I believe if you take it further and give of yourself, God will release not only His promises, but your life will be more fulfilled and you will live life abundantly.

You give but a little when you give your possessions. It is when you give of yourself that you truly give.

You are so blessed today that yesterday is jealous.

DAY 41

Keep God First & Share His Love

"And so we know and rely on the love God has for us. God is love. Whoever lives in love lives in God, and God in him."
(1 John 4:16)

When you put God first, you are establishing order for everything else in your life.

Your love has so much potential, to go so much further and build a greater foundation in your life.

Just as people grow and their lives change, we have to adapt our love to those changes, and our love has to mature and grow.

When you love people the way Christ loves you, you will start looking beyond their faults and shortcomings. You will start looking at their potential and the greatness that God has blessed all of us with, so we can bring out the best in all those we meet.

Love everyone, just as Christ loved you!

DAY 42

Are you a World Changer?

You may feel average today, but 1 John 4:4 says, *"You belong to God."* You are extremely valuable! Learn to recognize your value in who God made you to be and how He sees you.

You are a child of the Most High God!

We see in the book of James that faith without works is dead. Not only do you need to start doing something, you also have to say what God says about you, and then act on what you say.

"Yea, a man may say, Thou hast faith, and I have works: shew me thy faith without thy works, and I will shew thee my faith by my works." (James 2:18)

A lot of people say they are waiting on God. My question to you is, what if God is waiting on you?

THE ONES WHO ARE CRAZY ENOUGH TO THINK THEY CAN CHANGE THE WORLD, ARE USUALLY THE ONES WHO DO. - Steve Jobs

God has given you power to create wealth, in Jesus' Name!

DAY 43

Use Your Gifts

"In His grace, God has given us different gifts for doing certain things well."
(Romans 12:6)

How often we look upon God as our last and feeblest resource! We go to Him because we have nowhere else to go. And then we learn that the storms of life have driven us, not upon the rocks, but into the desired haven.

Use the gifts that He has given you so you can fulfill the purpose He called you to. You were created to be successful in business and in life. Period. Don't give up on your dreams because He has not given up on you.

"A man's gift maketh room for him, and bringeth him before great men." (Proverbs 18:16)

You are successful, in Jesus' Name!

DAY 43

Use Your Gifts

"In His grace, God has given us different gifts for doing certain things well."
(Romans 12:6)

How often we look upon God as our last and feeblest resource! We go to Him because we have nowhere else to go. And then we learn that the storms of life have driven us, not upon the rocks, but into the desired haven.

Use the gifts that He has given you so you can fulfill the purpose He called you to. You were created to be successful in business and in life. Period. Don't give up on your dreams because He has not given up on you.

"A man's gift maketh room for him, and bringeth him before great men." (Proverbs 18:16)

You are successful, in Jesus' Name!

DAY 44

Sing a Song of Praise

"Is any one of you in trouble? He should pray. Is anyone happy? Let him sing songs of praise."
(James 5:13)

Sing your way into healing, prosperity, joy and peace. Keep laughter in your life because it is like medicine, but better.

Seek to cultivate a buoyant, joyous sense of the crowded kindnesses of God in your daily life. When tests and trials come, count it all joy because as you trust in God, He will turn things around for your good. Some of you can't sing, but God said to make a joyful noise (Psalms 66:1). Break out into singing because as your praises go up, blessings come down to you.

"The Bible is a letter from God with our personal address on it." - Soren Kierkegaard

"For ye shall go out with joy, and be led forth with peace: the mountains and the hills shall break forth before you into singing, and all the trees of the field shall clap their hands."
(Isaiah 55:12)

You are blessed beyond measure, in Jesus' Name!

DAY 45

Prayer Changes Things

"The righteous shall flourish like the palm tree: he shall grow like a cedar in Lebanon. Those that are planted in the house of the LORD shall flourish in the courts of our God. They shall still bring forth fruit in old age; they shall be fat and flourishing…" (Psalm 92:12-14)

It is not too much to say that all real growth in the spiritual life–all victory over temptation, all confidence and peace in the presence of difficulties and dangers, all repose of spirit in times of great disappointment or loss, all habitual communion with God–depend upon the practice of secret prayer.

Prayer changes things. Practice this every day and God will open the windows of heaven and pour you out blessings that you will not have room enough to receive them. As He pours out these blessings, it is your responsibility to bless others. I have experienced this in my own life and I want you to experience the same or more!

"Again I say unto you, that if two of you shall agree on earth as touching anything that they shall ask, it shall be done for them of my Father which is in heaven." (Matthew 18:19)

The power of two or more touching and agreeing is very powerful. This is a promise of God so therefore you should rejoice and receive His blessings, in Jesus' Name!

DAY 46

You were Created to Win! Opposition Makes you Stronger!

There are times we all get discouraged because of opposition. No one likes to hear the word no. But just because you have opposition doesn't mean you're not in God's will. God is in control, and He's directing your steps. What's meant for your harm, God is going to use to your advantage.

Listen to what the Bible says in Romans 8.

"And we know that all things work together for good to them that love God, to them who are the called according to his purpose. For whom he did foreknow, he also did predestinate to be conformed to the image of his Son, that he might be the firstborn among many brethren. Moreover whom he did predestinate, them he also called: and whom he called, them he also justified: and whom he justified, them he also glorified. What shall we then say to these things? If God be for us, who can be against us?" (Romans 8:28-31)

No matter what comes your way, God is in control and there is nothing that can stop you from fulfilling your God given purpose and destiny. We are more than conquerors in Christ Jesus, because He is for us!

You are a winner, in Jesus' Name!

DAY 47

Just Believe

Do you need guidance in your life, wondering which way you should go?

Let me encourage you to pray a prayer that David prayed in Psalm 143: *"Show me the way I should go, for to You I lift up my soul....Teach me to do Your will, for You are my God; may Your good Spirit lead me on level ground"*
(vv. 8b, 10).

Don't worry if you do not see the results of your prayers right away, just know your prayers have already been answered. Now all you have to do is believe and receive.

The Bible says in Mark 11:24 *"Therefore I say unto you, what things soever ye desire, when ye pray, believe that ye receive them, and ye shall have them."*

Speak the Word, confess the Word, and receive His promises, in Jesus' Name!

DAY 48

Your Ideas are Just Ideas if they are Stuck in your Head

Get out of your head and step into your greatness!

God has given us all ideas. Now you have to get that idea out of your head, write it down and put it into action. In the book of Habakkuk, the word God says this: *"And the Lord answered me, and said, Write the vision, and make it plain upon tables, that he may run that readeth it."* (Habakkuk 2:2)

"You don't have to be great to get started, but you have to get started to become great." - Zig Ziglar

God never promised that we wouldn't have difficulties, but He did promise that He would give us strength for every battle and take what was meant for harm and use it to our advantage. You will succeed if you never give up. Most people get started but give up too soon. Winners never quit.

I believe you are a winner; and you will soar like an Eagle, in Jesus' Name!

DAY 49

Love Never Fails

You and I are human post offices. We are daily giving out messages of some sort to the world. They do not come from us, but through us; we do not create, we convey.

I've found the best way to convey a message is to share the word of God, which is the message of love. It is through love that God has given us the ability and desire to not only share His love, but to encourage others along the way.

"And now abideth faith, hope, charity, these three; but the greatest of these is charity." (1 Corinthians 13:13)

"Charity suffereth long, and is kind; charity envieth not; charity vaunteth not itself, is not puffed up, Doth not behave itself unseemly, seeketh not her own, is not easily provoked, thinketh no evil; Rejoiceth not in iniquity, but rejoiceth in the truth; Beareth all things, believeth all things, hopeth all things, endureth all things. Charity never faileth: but whether there be prophecies, they shall fail; whether there be tongues, they shall cease; whether there be knowledge, it shall vanish away." (1 Corinthians 13:4-8)

The main thing God is trying to convey to us is that **love never fails**!

DAY 50

The Power of Prayer & Praise

"Praise the Lord. Praise God in His sanctuary; praise Him in His mighty heavens.
Praise Him for His acts of power; praise Him for His surpassing greatness.
Praise Him with the sounding of the trumpet, praise Him with the harp and lyre,
praise Him with tambourine and dancing, praise Him with the strings and flute,
praise Him with the clash of cymbals, praise Him with resounding cymbals.
Let everything that has breath praise the Lord. Praise the Lord."
(Psalm 150:1-6)

The beauty of making a commitment to lifelong prayer with God is that your conversations with Him will never end–not even when you take your last breath here on earth.

Prayer will change your circumstances and any situation that you may be facing. Once you pray, start praising Him, because praise tear down walls and mountains, shut the mouths of lions, defeat giants and open doors that no one can shut.

When your praises go up, blessings come down.

God loves you and wants the best for you and so do I.

I pray blessings in your life, in Jesus' Name!

DAY 51

Share your Blessings

Nothing is really ours until we share it.

Do not let Satan deceive you into being afraid of God's plans for your life. Sow into others like others have sown unto you. The Bible says to give and it shall be given back to us, pressed down, shaken together and running over shall men give unto our bosom. You cannot out give God, because He owns it all anyway.

"Be devoted to one another with [authentic] brotherly affection [as members of one family], give preference to one another in honor; never lagging behind in diligence; aglow in the Spirit, enthusiastically serving the Lord; constantly rejoicing in hope [because of our confidence in Christ], steadfast and patient in distress, devoted to prayer [continually seeking wisdom, guidance, and strength], contributing to the needs of God's people, pursuing [the practice of] hospitality." (Romans 12:10-13)

You cannot out-give God!

Try Him and see.

He has blessed me more than I can ask or think. He will do it for you also, in Jesus' Name!!!

DAY 52

What Season Are You In?

"To everything there is a season, and a time to every purpose under the heaven: A time to be born, and a time to die; a time to plant, and a time to pluck up that which is planted; A time to kill, and a time to heal; a time to break down, and a time to build up; A time to weep, and a time to laugh; a time to mourn, and a time to dance; A time to cast away stones, and a time to gather stones together; a time to embrace, and a time to refrain from embracing; A time to get, and a time to lose; a time to keep, and a time to cast away; A time to rend, and a time to sew; a time to keep silence, and a time to speak; A time to love, and a time to hate; a time of war, and a time of peace." (Ecclesiastes 3:1-8)

My season is 24 hours a day and 365 days per year. It is a time to be blessed and to be a blessing.

It is a season to walk in divine health and prosperity every day of the year.
It is a season to walk in my divine destiny and purpose all year long and the years to come.
It is a season to walk in my calling and to be a light to all I come in contact with.
It is a season of Ephesians 3:20, more-than-I-can-ask-or-think Blessings.
It is a season of commanded blessings in my life because we have unity per Psalms 133.

If your seasons are like my seasons, say "Amen!"

DAY 53

Living a Fulfilled Life

People, places, and things were never meant to give us life. God alone is the author of a fulfilling life.

In prayer it is better to have a heart without words than words without a heart.

"For all the law is fulfilled in one word, even in this; Thou shalt love thy neighbour as thyself." (Galatians 5:14)

"Owe no man anything, but to love one another: for he that loveth another hath fulfilled the law." (Romans 13:8)

When God is your source, you will live a fulfilled abundant life, full of love, peace, joy, long suffering, gentleness, goodness, faith, meekness and temperance.

Much blessings, in Jesus' Name!

DAY 54

You are The Seed of Abraham

"For you are all sons of God through faith in Christ Jesus. For as many of you as were baptized into Christ have put on Christ. There is neither Jew nor Greek, there is neither slave nor free, there is neither male nor female; for you are all one in Christ Jesus. And if you are Christ's then you are Abraham's seed, and heirs according to the promise."
(Galatians 3:26-29)

Because we are joint heirs with Christ, we are blessed with all the seeds of Abraham. This is a promise from God Almighty. We need to walk in and receive these blessings that were promised to each and every one of us.

The Bible says the wealth of the wicked is laid up for the just (Proverbs 13:22). I believe the greatest transformation of wealth is happening now and it is important for those that believe, to walk in agreement to fulfill His purpose and destiny in our lives. There is power in unity and agreement. If two or three shall touch and agree, nothing is impossible to those that believe. Remember, you are the seed of Abraham, therefore the promise is to you and me.

The promise is for you and all your family, in Jesus' Name!

DAY 55

Rejoice

"Rejoice in the Lord always; again I will say, Rejoice."
(Philippians 4:4)

Faith is an activity; it is something that has to be applied.

If you have faith, you will have: Strength, rest, guidance, grace, help, sympathy, highly favored, anointed and appointed, abundantly blessed, prosperous, victorious, love-all from God to us.

What a list of blessings!

If I were you, I would start rejoicing and praising Him for all of these wonderful blessings.

DAY 56

Be Content in Today; Tomorrow You will See Great Gain

"But Godliness with contentment is great gain." (1 Timothy 6:6)

"Let your conversation be without covetousness; and be content with such things as ye have: for he hath said, I will never leave thee, nor forsake thee." (Hebrews 13:5)

Be the best that you can today and you will grow into what you are going to be tomorrow.
Accept not just who you are, but also the season God has you in right now!

Being content in where God has you right now in life, just means you are about to leap and be propelled to a whole new level in your life because He wants the best for you. It is normal for your tomorrows to be better than your yesterday's.

You need to expect that each day will be better than before. Now I pray for you, my family and friends that you will be blessed and everyday all things become new. Your future is bright and everyone that you meet, you will become a light in their eyes. You will become an example for others to follow as you put your trust totally in God.

Amen and Amen!

DAY 57

Bless People with your Compliments

"The words of a man's mouth are as deep waters; the wellspring of wisdom is as a flowing brook." (Proverbs 18:4)

"A gentle tongue is a tree of life...." (Proverbs 15:4)

Your words bring healing by speaking blessings in people's lives.

When you're kind, encouraging and free with your compliments, when you don't just think something good but you take time to verbalize it in the lives of those around you, not only are you being a healer, but you help others become everything God has created them to be. As you help others rise higher, God is going to cause you to rise higher!

People respond to praise, not criticism.

"How sweet are your words to my taste, sweeter than honey to my mouth!" (Psalm 119:103).

What you say, and how you say it, is very important. Build people up with positive words!

DAY 58

Are you an Entrepreneur?

"Wealth and riches are in his house; and his righteousness endureth forever." (Psalms 112:3)

"A good man leaveth an inheritance to his children's children; And the wealth of the sinner is laid up for the righteous." (Proverbs 13:22)

When I think of these two scriptures, I think of the word "Entrepreneur" which means freedom, to have the ability to express yourself and put your ideas to work, to fulfill your dreams without being hindered. They are passionate about what they are doing and enjoy doing it.

In order to leave an inheritance for your children's Children, you have to be in a financial position to do so.

Let's work together to fulfill the purpose we were called to do and be.

The real "you" was created to succeed and live an abundant life!

DAY 59

Do You Have and Walk in His Promises?

"As soon as Jesus heard the word that was spoken, he saith unto the ruler of the synagogue, be not afraid, only believe."
(Mark 5:36)

He is saying to you also, only believe!

1. Do you believe you can achieve your dreams?
2. Do you believe that you are more than a conqueror?
3. Do you believe you can fulfill your destiny?
4. Do you believe that you can become the lender and not the borrower?
5. Do you believe that you can become a better giver?
6. Do you believe that you can live in abundance?
7. Do you believe that you walk in divine healing?
8. Do you believe that you are blessed to be a blessing?
9. Do you believe that all your needs are met according to His riches in glory?
10. Do you believe that you are joint heirs with Christ?

I believe you have all of these and every other promise from God, in Jesus' Name!

DAY 60

He Knows your Heart

"Rejoice always; pray without ceasing; in everything give thanks: for this is the will of God in Christ Jesus toward you." (1 Thessalonians 5:16-18)

When you can't put your prayers into words, God hears your heart.

When you are faced in difficult situations or circumstances, let the good outweigh the bad. There will always be negative things that come against you, but choose to be grateful where God has you right now and you will see things change.

Gratitude as a discipline involves a conscious choice. I can choose to be grateful even when my emotions and feelings are still steeped in hurt and resentment. It is amazing how many occasions present themselves in which I can choose gratitude instead of a complaint.

"Search me, O God, and know my heart: Try me, and know my thoughts;" (Psalms 139:23)

He loves you; and so do I!

FROM US TO YOU

A special letter from Minister Leon Johnson and Diamond Johnson is now available!

Scan the QR Code, type the URL into your browser, or click the link (in the eBook) to access the message:

https://subscribepage.io/volume1thankyouletter

Congratulations on Completing the 60-Day Devotional Journey!

If you've walked through the 60-Day Devotional, you've already built a rhythm of faith worth sharing. These group leader resources are designed to help you explore the possibility of gathering friends, family, or a small group—without turning the devotional into a lesson or adding pressure to teach. And remember: this is just the beginning!

Scan the QR Code, type the URL into your browser, or click the link (in the eBook) to download these devotional-aligned group resources.

https://subscribepage.io/volume1groupresourcehub

FOR MINISTRY LEADERS & PASTORS:

If you've journeyed through this devotional as a leader, you may be sensing its potential to serve more than individuals—it can help cultivate unity, rhythm, and spiritual alignment across a church community without becoming another program. This resource offers gentle insight into how churches are using the devotional together and invites leaders to prayerfully discern next steps at their own pace.

Scan the QR Code, type the URL into your browser, or click the link (in the eBook) to explore church-centered guidance and next steps.

https://subscribepage.io/volume1churchresourcehub

About the Authors: A Father-Daughter Duo

Minister Leon Johnson

Diamond Johnson

With a heart for helping the called and chosen walk confidently in their God-given purpose, Minister Leon Johnson leads LifeTime Inspirations Ministries and writes to equip believers with truth, power, and Biblical clarity.

His daughter, Diamond Johnson, co-writes and edits each of the devotionals to assist with simplifying and amplifying the messages. Together, they aim to inspire and motivate both new and seasoned believers to draw closer to God and live according to the Word.

AFTERWORD

We want to take this opportunity to thank you all for your love and support! It's because of you that we are able to bring the gospel to all corners of the world, blessing everyone with God's love in action!

Now that you have completed volume 1, what's next? **The LifeTime Inspirations 60-Day Devotional Volume 2 E-Book** will be released soon! If you subscribe to our E-newsletter, you'll get a discount on the Volume 2 E-Book Bundle Pre-Order! You can subscribe here to know when Volume 2 will drop.

https://preview.mailerlite.io/forms/1472749/173544436619281685/share

AFTERWORD

Also, don't forget to leave a review on our site or on Amazon; and follow us on social media for more inspirational messages and a sneak peek into Volume 2's messages!

Follow us on Instagram/Threads: @lifetimeinspire

Subscribe to Our YouTube Channel: @lifetimeinspirationsofficial

Follow us on Tiktok: @lifetimeinspirations

Follow us on Facebook: @lifetimeinspirationsofficial